INTRODUCTION

Just lately we have had quite a few letters asking about Andy's age.

For Pub Quiz and Trivia purposes, he's only Thirty years old – having first appeared in print in 1957.

His real age, we don't know and wouldn't enquire. It's a dangerous subject, only second to asking Florrie hers.

Mind you, when he occasionally grabs the pepper and salt and says "There was Rommel and there was me – " you can put two and two together.

Percy puts it around that the only battling Capp ever did was to be first in the NAAFI queue. Pure spite.

It's a well known fact that Percy has always had a thing about Flo and can't get over her choosing our hero.

He's still very attractive to women – he mentioned it only the other week – and Flo's still very attractive too, especially on pay days.

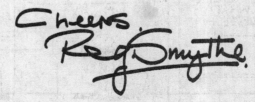

Cheers.
Reg Smythe.

BUMP BUMP

"RACING

TCH-!

ABSOLUTELY USELESS, THIS WOMAN — I HAVE TO DO *EVERYTHING* FOR HER

I'M IN THE TRADE MYSELF. WHAT'S YOUR CLIENTELE LIKE?

SORT OF MIXED —

THAT COUPLE FOR INSTANCE, THEY'RE IN THE LOWER-INCOME, UPPER-OUTGO GROUP

U206

U207

U214

Smythe

U215

U218

— I WASN'T VERY WELL PLACED, BUT I POTTED THE BLUE BALL—

YOU CAN TELL THEY AREN'T MARRIED...

— AND ROLLED NICELY ON TO THE PINK—

TALK TO Y'SELF, I'M GOING TO SIT WITH MUM!

NOTHING ANNOYS 'EM SO MUCH AS TO HAVE SOMEONE GO RIGHT ON TALKING WHEN THEY'RE INTERRUPTING

Smythe

READY, FOLKS?

I THOUGHT WE'D BE GOING OUT IN A FOURSOME, FLO — ISN'T ANDY FREE?

U219

HE COULDN'T MAKE IT, ADA. COUNT YOURSELVES LUCKY—

NOTHING'S MORE EXPENSIVE THAN MY LAD BEING FREE FOR THE EVENING

THANKS FOR THE TIP

Smythe

U220

U221

U224

Panel 1: ANY DECISION YET, MUM?

Panel 2: YES, FLO. THANKS ALL THE SAME, BUT I'VE DECIDED TO LEAVE IT FOR ANOTHER YEAR

Panel 3: CAN'T BLAME HER. NOTHING MAKES YOU FEEL THAT YOUR HOME IS YOUR *CASTLE* MORE THAN GETTING AN ESTIMATE FROM MY LAD TO HAVE IT PAINTED

U225

Panel 4: TCH, FLIPPIN' DEPRESSING. THE MORE I READ THE PAPERS THE MORE I THINK ABOUT EMIGRATING—

Panel 5: THERE'S SOMETHING YOU SHOULD KNOW, PAL — THEY WON'T ACCEPT YOU UNLESS YOU PROVE THAT YOU CAN SUPPORT Y'SELF

Panel 6: SO? *YOU'D* BE COMING WITH ME, WOULDN'T YOU?

ANY OTHER NEWS, FLO?

HIS LORDSHIP IS THREATENING TO LEAVE ME AGAIN, MUM — CAN YOU IMAGINE HIM TRYING TO SURVIVE WITHOUT *ME*?

OH, I DON'T KNOW, FLO. HE'S PRETTY RESOURCEFUL THAT WAY —

THANKS, MISSUS

— A TWIT CAN ALWAYS FIND A BIGGER TWIT TO SUPPORT HIM

U232

I BET YOU DIDN'T WEED THAT BACK GARDEN LIKE YOU PROMISED —

U233

I DID, Y'KNOW. I'VE COMPLETELY CLEARED THAT BIT BY THE SHED

OH, *NO!* THAT'S WHERE I PLANTED MY FORGET-ME-NOTS!

SORRY, PET, I FORGOT

Panel 1: WELL? WHAT DO YOU THINK? WE'VE GOT TO DO SOMETHING

Panel 2: DON'T RUSH ME, PET —

U256

Panel 3: I MAKE A POINT OF LOOKING AT EVERY ISSUE FROM EVERY ANGLE

Panel 4: HE *WOULD* DO — IT MAKES 'EM EASIER TO SIDE-STEP

Panel 5: A PINT OF BITTER AND A HALF OF LAGER, JACKIE —

U257

Panel 6: OH, DEAR, I'VE COME OUT WITHOUT MY WALLET

Panel 7: DON'T WORRY ABOUT IT —

Panel 8: COMING OUT WITHOUT OUR MONEY ISN'T THE DRAG IT USED TO BE — NOW WE CAN ENJOY JOGGING BACK HOME TO GET IT, EH?

U266

U267

WHAT ARE YOU BUYING HIM FOR CHRISTMAS, FLO?

I DON'T KNOW, MOTHER — ANY IDEAS?

U268

WELL, I WAS THINKING OF GETTING HIM ONE OF THOSE BOOKS ABOUT HOW TO BE A SUCCESS

FORGET IT, MUM, I'VE GOT ENOUGH TO DO — HE'D HAVE ME READING IT TO HIM

Z

YOU NEVER SAY YOU LOVE ME —

U269

DO I NEED TO, PET? I'M SPENDING THE EVENING AT HOME WITH YOU, AREN'T I? I COULD BE OUT WITH THE LADS, Y'KNOW

AND I'M QUITE CERTAIN THAT HIS DECISION HAD ABSOLUTELY NOTHING TO DO WITH HIM WANTING TO SEE THE BOXING ON TELLY

NO MATTER WHAT YOU SAY, MUM, I'M STILL GOING BACK HOME TO HIM. HE MUST BE RUNNING INTO ALL KINDS OF PROBLEMS BY NOW

HE'LL GET BY, FLO. HE'S GOT A HEAD ON HIS SHOULDERS

EXACTLY—

AND KNOWING THAT LAD, I BET IT'S A DIFFERENT ONE EVERY NIGHT

U270

Smythe

IF YOU ASK ME, YOU'RE A BIT TOO HARD ON THAT LASS OF YOURS, ERIC. MIND YOU, YOU'RE STILL YOUNG—

U271

YOU'LL LEARN. WHEN YOU GET MARRIED YOU'LL FIND THAT MOST BUST-UPS CAN BE AVOIDED—

I'M SITTING OUT HERE LIKE A LEMON, PET, DRINKING ON MY OWN. WHEN ARE YOU GOING TO PUT THAT CUE AWAY?

Smythe

WHEN I'M GOOD AND READY!!

U276

U277

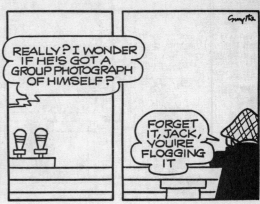

U286

NEW SUIT YOU'RE WEARING, ANDY?

NO, IT'S ONE I'VE HAD FOR YEARS. I JUST GAVE IT A PRESS AND IT CAME UP A TREAT

YOU REALLY DID IT *YOURSELF*?

I REALLY DID...

IF YOU'RE INTERESTED, THE BEST WAY TO LEARN HOW TO DO SOMETHING YOURSELF IS TO CRITICISE THE WAY YOUR MISSUS IS DOING IT

GOT NASTY, EH?

ALES

BAR

I'M WAITING TO LOCK UP, ANDY. I TRUST YOU'RE NOT GOING TO MAKE THE MISTAKE OF TRYING MY PATIENCE AGAIN TONIGHT?

U287

COULD BE

THUMP

WALLOP

PEOPLE WHO NEVER MAKE THE SAME MISTAKE TWICE MISS A HELLUVA LOT OF FUN, EH, JACK?

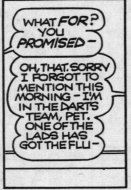

TONIGHT
GREYHOUND
RACING

U296

ME AND FLO HAD A
HELLUVA ROW BEFORE
I LEFT HOME — SHE
WANTED ME TO TAKE
HER TO THE
PICTURES...

WHY DIDN'T
SHE
INSIST ?!

GOOD LUCK, LAD.
HOPE YOU ENJOY
THE EXPERIENCE

THANKS,
MISTER

TAKE
IT
EASY,
ANDY

I DON'T
KNOW
WHAT
YOU'RE
ON
ABOUT

THE FIRST THING THAT
STRIKES A NEWCOMER
TO OUR LEAGUE IS
GENERALLY CAPP

U297

STILL REFUSE TO TELL ME WHERE YOUR DOLE MONEY WENT?

...THAT'S RIGHT—

THUMP

YOU SHOULD SEE HER WHEN I *TELL* HER

U300

Smythe

HE WON'T BE COMING HOME AT *THIS* TIME OF NIGHT— HE KNOWS HOW MAD YOU'LL BE...

HE'LL PROBABLY SLIP IN AFTER YOU'VE GONE TO WORK IN THE MORNING...

DON'T BE DAFT, NOT *HIM*....

AT HIS TIME OF LIFE, COMING HOME IS THE ONLY BIT OF ADVENTURE LEFT

U301

Smythe

AW, C'MON, PET, IT'S A RACING CERTAINTY

U306

OH, YES? YOU'VE BACKED IT AT LEAST HALF A DOZEN TIMES AND IT'S NEVER COME IN THE FIRST THREE

IT'S BOUND TO WIN THIS TIME, FLO. THE CONDITIONS ARE JUST RIGHT FOR IT

I WISH HE WAS AS LOYAL TO ME AS HE IS TO THAT FLIPPIN' HORSE

STOP MOANING. IT'S A CONTACT SPORT — RIGHT?

U307

WRONG. WHEN CAPP'S PLAYING IT'S A COLLISION SPORT

YOU'RE HOME EARLY, PET

I'M GOING FISHING IN THE MORNING. I'VE ASKED YOUR MOTHER TO COME AND GIVE ME A SHOUT AT FIVE

V16

THE NERVE OF YOU

NOT AT ALL. SHE'S DONE SO MANY DIRTY TRICKS IN HER TIME, I DOUBT IF SHE GETS ANY SLEEP, ANYWAY

Smythe

V17

I'M READY TO LOCK UP, ANDY—

WHAT'VE YOU GOT PLANNED FOR US NOW — A DISCO OR SOMETHING?

OH, LET ME THINK NOW...

?

WELL—?

?

POOR LITTLE DEVIL. HE FINDS IT A WHOLE LOT EASIER TO CHARM THE YOUNG 'UNS THAN KNOW WHAT TO DO WITH 'EM

Smythe

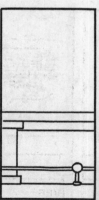

BINGO

YIPPEE!

V36

OH-OHH

HI, PET

HI, PET

CLICK

TCH! TCH! JUST LOOK AT THAT, FLO—!

AR

V37

LEAVE IT BE, RUBE. AT *HIS* AGE HE HAS TO HOLD ON TO *SOMETHING*

YOUR MISSUS?

WHO ELSE?

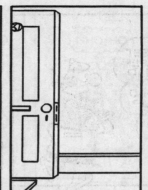

SOMETIMES I THINK HE'S NEVER GOING TO COME HOME TO ME AGAIN. THEN I THINK HE WILL. IN EITHER CASE, IT CALLS FOR A BRANDY

Smythe

♪♪♪!!!!

EVERYTHING COMES TO HE WHO TRIES TO ENFORCE THE RULES

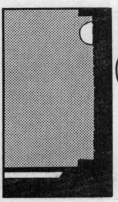

V46

V47

V52

V53

I FEEL REAL GUILTY. WE SHOULDN'T BE OUT SPENDING THE RENT - PERCY WILL BE ROUND FOR IT TODAY

STOP WORRYING, PET. HE WON'T COME - HE'D BE CRAZY TO TURN OUT IN WEATHER LIKE THIS

YOU'RE PROBABLY RIGHT - LET'S HOPE HE'LL BE SENSIBLE LIKE US, EH?

V70

I WOULDN'T MIND COMING ON THAT TRIP TO LONDON WITH YOU AND CHALKIE - HOW ABOUT IT?

DEPENDS ON CIRCUMSTANCES

WHAT CIRCUMSTANCES?

HERS

V71

I'VE GOT A REAL LOAD OF SHOPPING TO HUMP BACK FROM THE MARKET

I RECKON THE CREATOR SHOULD HAVE MADE HOUSEWIVES WITH FOUR ARMS, EH, PET?

V72

HE *DID,* MATE—

BUT THE OTHER TWO ARE ON THEIR HUSBANDS

STOP PUSHING

NO MATTER WHAT YOUR TROUBLE IS, PERCY, ALWAYS REMEMBER THAT ANDY IS ON YOUR SIDE

AND ALWAYS THE SIDE HE CARRIES HIS SATCHEL ON

V73

DON'T CHANGE YOUR MIND, PET — *I NEED YOU!* RUBE'S BEEN LETTING ME OVERSLEEP AT OPENING TIME

V76

TCH! TRUST *HER*

THEY'VE GOT TO FEEL NEEDED. IF YOU CAN'T GIVE 'EM A GOOD REASON, THEY'LL BE SATISFIED WITH A BAD ONE

THERE YOU ARE, PERCY, PLUS A BIT OFF THE ARREARS

RENT

IT MAKES ME MAD, PAYING OUT RENT EVERY WEEK — IF WE'D BOUGHT THE HOUSE WHEN WE HAD THE CHANCE WE WOULD OWN IT BY NOW—!

V77

MAKE YOUR MIND UP, WOMAN —

YOU'RE ALWAYS RABBITING ON ABOUT WHAT A DUMP WE'RE LIVING IN — NOW YOU WISH WE *OWNED* IT

NOTHING PERSONAL, SPORT

JUST DOING YOUR JOB, PAL

THERE'S A BOWLING ALLEY NEXT DOOR, AND WHEN I START GETTING COMPLAINTS FROM *THEM* ABOUT THE NOISE IN *HERE*—

V78

HOW'S CHALKIE, RUBE? MUST HAVE BEEN AFTER TWELVE WHEN ANDY GOT IN LAS'NIGHT—

MY HUSBAND HAS KEPT REGULAR HOURS FOR YEARS

OH, DEAR, I AM SORRY—WHAT'S HE IN FOR?

WEL-LL, SANCTIMONIOUS TWIT

V79

SEE YOU, PET

SEE YOU

C'MON, CHALKIE, GET A MOVE ON

IF YOU INSIST

WE NEED OUR BRAINS TESTING, GOING OUT ON A NIGHT LIKE THIS

I FEEL THE SAME AS YOU, CHALKIE. BUT YOU KNOW HOW IT IS – IF WE STAYED IN *ONE* NIGHT THEY'D EXPECT US TO STAY IN *EVERY* NIGHT

THAT'S A FACT

ALES

V80

V81

YOU HAVEN'T SAID ANYTHING ABOUT THE GAME –

I'M JUST NATURALLY MODEST

THERE'LL BE A REPORT IN THE LOCAL PAPER, IF YOU'RE INTERESTED

WELL, *SORT* OF MODEST – HE JUST PREFERS PEOPLE TO FIND OUT FOR THEMSELVES HOW WONDERFUL HE IS

HOW DO YOU RATE MY CHANCES, JACK?

FINE, ANDY, FINE—

NEVER UNDERESTIMATE THE LACK OF TASTE OF THE BUYING PUBLIC, EH?

WATCH YOUR MOUTH, JACKIE

THANKS A MILLION, VICAR. YOU'VE MADE ME A VERY 'APPY MAN INDEED

IT WON'T BUY YOU TRUE HAPPINESS, ANDY

THAT'S OKAY. YOU KNOW ME — I'M EASILY FOOLED

WHAT'S NEW, SANDRA?

NOT A LOT, DEAR — EXCEPT THAT HIS LORDSHIP HERE IS TOYING WITH THE IDEA OF HAVING A TELEPHONE INSTALLED

V108

...IT'D BE LOVELY TO TALK TO HIM WITHOUT HAVING TO BUY HIM A DRINK

SHADDAP

Smythe

ARE WE GOING TO THE LOCAL?

SURE. WHY NOT?

V109

CAN'T WE GO SOME PLACE WHERE WE'LL BE ALONE? YOU KNOW WHAT IT'S LIKE IN THERE —

DAVEY COMES UP TALKING ABOUT SNOOKER, BILLY WANTS YOU TO PLAY DOMINOES, AND ERIC SAYS HOW ABOUT A GAME OF DARTS —

LOOK, PET, IF YOU WANT TO BE ALONE, WHY DON'T YOU STAY AT HOME?

Smythe

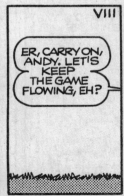

SOME BOYFRIEND YOU'VE GOT, DEAR!

ME? I DON'T EVEN KNOW HIM – I THOUGHT HE WAS WITH YOU

HOW ARE YOU FINDING LIFE IN THIS LEAGUE, SON?

IT HAS ITS MOMENTS, MISTER CAPP –

V117

– ALL OF THEM HORRIBLE

IT'S NO USE, DEAR, I'VE A CONFESSION TO MAKE — I'M A MARRIED MAN....

SNIFF

V120

FUNNY HOW HE ALWAYS GETS THESE BOUTS OF INTEGRITY AROUND THE TIME IT'S HIS TURN TO GET THE DRINKS IN

Smythe

IF YOU'D CARE TO JOIN ME, I THOUGHT WE MIGHT TIDY UP MUM'S GARDEN AN' GIVE HER A NICE SURPRISE WHEN SHE ARRIVES BACK FROM HOLIDAY

ME? AFTER ALL THE THINGS I'VE SAID ABOUT HER?

V121

YOUR CONSCIENCE WON'T LET YOU?

SOMETHING LIKE THAT

HIS CONSCIENCE REALLY COMES ALIVE WHEN ANYTHING CROPS UP THAT SOUNDS A BIT LIKE WORK

Smythe

I'M FED UP. I'LL NEVER GET ANYWHERE IN THIS TOWN —

V132

I'VE HALF A MIND TO GET MESELF AWAY — SEEK MY FORTUNE WHILE THERE'S STILL TIME

WELL, YOU'VE HAD PLENTY OF PRACTICE — YOU'VE BEEN AFTER *MINE* FOR LONG ENOUGH

HOW LONG HAS IT BEEN, DEAR?

ALMOST FIVE YEARS —

HOW LONG WAS *YOUR* ENGAGEMENT, FLO?

IT WASN'T REALLY AN ENGAGEMENT, DEAR, MORE OF A SKIRMISH

V133

FLO! JUST CALLED BY TO SEE HOW YOU'RE GETTING ALONG WITHOUT ME ..... INCIDENTALLY, COULD YOU LEND —

YOU KNOW WHAT *YOU* CAN DO

ANY MORE OF YOUR LIP AND I'LL COME BACK TO YOU—!!

V140

HELP Y'SELF

REMEMBER, NOW, I WANT YOU TO BEHAVE Y'SELF AT THE RECEPTION

YES, PET

READY, FOLKS?

CHALKIE ISN'T COMING, FLO — HE SAYS WEDDINGS DEPRESS HIM

THEY DON'T BOTHER *THIS* LAD. HE'S THE CAREFREE TYPE — HE DOESN'T *CARE* AS LONG AS THE BOOZE IS *FREE*

V141

I SAID NO! I PROMISED PERCY I'D PAY TWO POUNDS OFF THE ARREARS THIS WEEK AND I'M NOT GOING BACK ON MY WORD!

YES. BUT THAT'S STILL BETTER THAN HAVING TO PAY THE WHOLE RENT, ISN'T IT, PET?

IT'S AS WELL AS THE RENT, DUMBBELL!

V142

HE LIVES IN A WORLD OF HIS OWN

YOU SWORE YOU'D STAY WITH ME FOR GOOD THIS TIME—

I CAN'T RELY ON YOU. YOU'RE JUST NOT DEPENDABLE

I SUPPOSE YOU ARE?

YES, I AM!

SORT OF. EVER SINCE HE WAS OLD ENOUGH TO WORK, HE HASN'T

V143

V148

V149

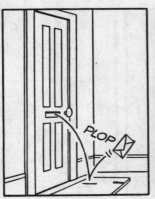

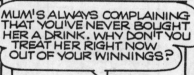

V174

V175

V186

V187

HOW ARE YOU FINDING MARRIED LIFE, DEAR?

I FIND THERE'S A LOT OF ADJUSTING TO DO, FLO, AND LOTS OF DIFFERENCES TO BE SETTLED

V190

I KNOW HOW IT IS, DEAR

WE SETTLED ALL *OUR* DIFFERENCES IN THE FIRST FEW MONTHS. EVER SINCE THEN WE'VE JUST BEEN HAMMERING OUT THE PRACTICAL DETAILS

CITIZENS ADVICE

AH, WELL, TIME TO OPEN UP...

EVERY MORNING, THE SAME OLD ARGUMENT —WHOSE TURN IS IT TO BUY THE DRINKS

V191

CAN I BUY YOU A DRINK, DEAR?

NO, THANKS, I'M OKAY. BUT YOU CAN COME AND CHAT AND TELL ME WHAT YOU'VE BEEN UP TO LATELY

WHAT DO YOU RECKON, JACK?

SAME AS YOU. STEER CLEAR OF THE LASS WHO COMES INTO A PUB TO LISTEN AND NOT TO DRINK

TOO TRUE

I'M OFF HOME, CHALKIE. GOOD NIGHT, JACK

WHAT'S UP WITH *HIM?* IT'S NOT LIKE ANDY TO SEE A PRETTY LASS AT THE BAR WITHOUT TRYING HIS LUCK

REPLACED AS FOOTBALL CAPTAIN, LEFT OUT OF THE DARTS TEAM — HE COULDN'T RISK *ANOTHER* REJECTION

© 1987 Mirror Publications Ltd.
First published in Great Britain by Mirror Publications Ltd., Athene House, 66/73 Shoe Lane, London EC4P 4AB
Colour printing by Creative Print & Design, Harmondsworth, Middx. Printed in Great Britain by Spottiswoode Ballantyne Printers Ltd.,
Colchester and London. Distributed by Odhams Distribution Ltd., London. Tel: 01-831 8288
ISBN 0 85939 494 8